Good Food

I Like Berries

By Jennifer Julius

Welcome
Books

Children's Press
A Division of Grolier Publishing
New York / London / Hong Kong / Sydney
Danbury, Connecticut

Photo Credits: Cover, pp. 5, 7, 9, 11, 15, 17, 19, 21 by Maura Boruchow; p. 13 © IndexStock
Contributing Editor: Jeri Cipriano
Book Design: Nelson Sa

Visit Children's Press on the Internet at:
http://publishing.grolier.com

Library of Congress Cataloging-in-Publication Data

Julius, Jennifer.
   I like berries / by Jennifer Julius.
   p. cm. – (Good food)
   Includes bibliographical references and index.
   ISBN 0-516-23129-4 (lib. bdg.) – ISBN 0-516-23054-9 (pbk.)
   1. Cookery (Berries)—Juvenile literature. 2. Berries—Juvenile literature. [1. Berries.] I.
Title. II. Series.

TX813.B4 J85 2000
641.6'47—dc21

00-043069

Contents

I like berries.

Do you like berries?

There are many kinds
of berries.

What are these small, blue berries?

They are blueberries!

Blueberries taste great baked in a **muffin**.

7

What are these berries with the tiny **seeds**?

They are strawberries!

Strawberries taste great in ice cream.

9

What are these soft, red berries?

They are raspberries!

Raspberries taste great with cereal.

11

What are these black berries that grow in the wild?

They are blackberries!

Blackberries taste great right off the bush.

13

What are these hard, red berries?

They are cranberries!

Cranberries taste great when cooked to make sauce.

What are these tiny, black berries?

They look like **raisins.** But they are currants!

Currants taste great as jelly.

17

Look at all the ways you can eat berries!

Which kind of berries do you like to eat?

New Words

muffin (**muf-in**) a kind
of small cake

raisins (**ray**-zinz) sweet
dried grapes

seeds (**seedz**) the small
parts of plants

To Find Out More

Books
Fruit
by Jillian Powell
Raintree Steck-Vaughn Publishers

Oliver's Fruit Salad
by Vivian French
Orchard Books

Web Site
The Cranberry Lady
http://www.thecranberrylady.com/
Meet the cranberry lady and learn how and where
cranberries grow. Read about all the foods you
can make with cranberries.

23

Index

About the Author

Jennifer Julius is a freelance writer and editor who specializes in educational publishing. She lives in New York City.

Reading Consultants

Kris Flynn, Coordinator, Small School District Literacy, The San Diego County Office of Education

Shelly Forys, Certified Reading Recovery Specialist, W.J. Zahnow Elementary School, Waterloo, IL

Peggy McNamara, Professor, Bank Street College of Education, Reading and Literacy Program